Sea View Camping

THE WEST COUNTRY

Vicarious Media

Derived from a guide first published in Great Britain by Brian M. Leahy, 2006. Reprinted 2007.
Republished 2008 and 2010 by Vicarious Books Ltd.
This variant published 2016 by Vicarious Media.

Vicarious Media, 62 Tontine Street, Folkestone, Kent, CT20 1JP. Tel: 0131 2083333

Editors: Chris Doree, Pami Hoggatt, Benjamin Taylor and Meli George

Design and artwork by: Chris Gladman Design Tel: 07745 856652

Front cover
Main picture: Ayr Holiday Park, Cornwall.
Small pictures: Manor Farm, Devon and Golden Cap, Dorset.

Back cover
Small pictures: Beacon Cottage, Cornwall and Putsborough Sands, Devon.

The following symbols identify amenities that are either on site or within five minutes' walk, unless otherwise indicated. The facilities have not been tested and charges may apply.

⊟ Pub/bar

⊞ Shop

ℚ Beach

⚓ Slipway

⚐ Indoor or outdoor swimming pool

⚠ Children's play area

⚲ Footpath

9 **Information Symbols**

Cost – The cost of the campsite is indicated by the £ symbols. All prices are based on two people in one caravan or motorhome with electric during August. Prices are offered as a guideline only and should always be confirmed in advance.

£ Up to £10 per night

££ £10-17 per night

£££ £17-35 per night

££££ £35 or more per night

🐕 Many campsites allow dogs on site, indicated by the dog symbol, but confirmation must always be sought in advance that your dog(s) can be accommodated. Many campsites charge extra for dogs, there may be a limit on the number of dogs allowed on site, and some sites specify the type of units that dogs can be accommodated in. Some sites also have breed restrictions, so always check your breed is permitted before arrival. Campsite owners and other holidaymakers expect dogs to be kept quiet and under control, and usually on a lead, at all times. Dogs must be exercised in appropriate areas, or offsite, and all mess must be cleared in a responsible fashion. In addition, it is advised that you never leave your dog unattended.

♥♥ This symbol refers to adult only campsites. No person under the age of 18 will be admitted.

Ⓜ This symbol refers to member only campsites. Generally these belong to either the Camping and Caravanning Club or the Caravan Club and a valid membership is required to stay, though it may be possible to join at reception. The name of the club is usually indicated in the title of the campsite. CS and CL sites are also for members only.

CS (Certified Sites) - These sites are for Camping and Caravanning Club members only. These are small sites, restricted to five caravans or motorhomes, plus tents space permitting.

CL (Certified Locations) - These sites are for Caravan Club members only. These are small sites, restricted to five caravans or motorhomes.

ⓘ Internet available (charges may apply).

WiFi WiFi available (charges may apply).

10 **Directions** – Directions are provided. Please note that many campsites near the sea are down narrow lanes with passing places.

11 **Awards** – English tourist board awarded star ratings.

12 **GPS Coordinates** – Coordinates are presented in true GPS format. Our office, for example, is located at N51°04.895' E001°10.978'. You may need to select this format in your navigator's menu. Coordinates were recorded at the site entrance, or sometimes the approach road/driveway, to prevent navigator error. We have provided directions that should be suitable for most vehicles but your navigator may not, so ensure that you check the route against a map and our directions. Please note that postcodes often do not provide accurate destinations when used with satellite navigators.

13 **OS grid references** – The six figure grid references provided refer to locations on the Ordinance Survey Landranger 1:50,000 sheet map series. The first three numbers and the two letters refer to the map identification code. The remaining numbers create a six-digit grid reference. Unlike the GPS coordinates, these will locate the campsite rather than the entrance.

14 **Opening dates** – Opening dates change year to year and are given as an indication only, please check with the campsite before arrival.

15 **Advanced booking** – You will need to contact the individual campsites to make advanced bookings, especially if you are planning a visiting during the summer holidays or other peak periods.

Abbreviations

mins = minutes   sp = signposted

Vicarious Shop

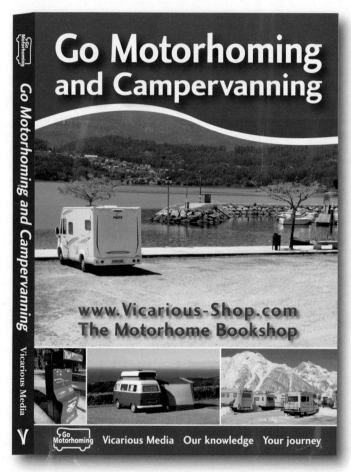

Cornish Tin Mine

Vicarious Shop

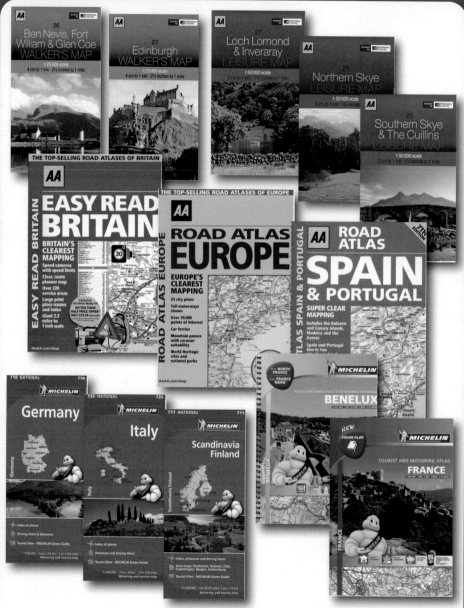

Don't get lost, get your maps from www.Vicarious-Shop.com. Extensive range of road atlases and sheet maps for the UK and Europe all sold at RRP with free UK P&P.

To order, give us a call or visit our website to buy online.

Tel: 0131 2083333   www.Vicarious-Shop.com

Coast Path, Land's End, Cornwall

Beach Barbecue

Vicarious Shop

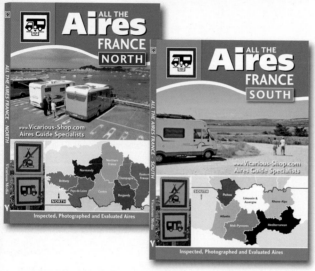

Motorhomers and campervanners have the privilege of stopping overnight all over Europe at stopovers known as Aires. For more information, visit www.all-the-aires.co.uk.

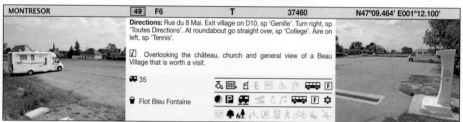

MONTRESOR		49	F6	T	37460	N47°09.464' E001°12.100'

Directions: Rue du 8 Mai. Exit village on D10, sp 'Genille'. Turn right, sp 'Toutes Directions'. At roundabout go straight over, sp 'College'. Aire on left, sp 'Tennis'.

ℹ️ Overlooking the château, church and general view of a Beau Village that is worth a visit.

🚐 35

💧 Flot Bleu Fontaine

Sample France entry with corresponding mapping. Similar mapping for Spain and Portugal and Belgium, Luxembourg and Holland.

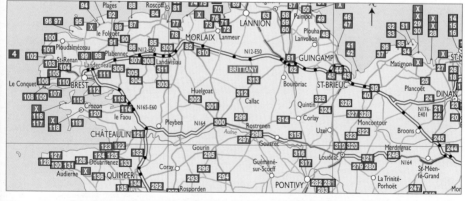

To order, give us a call or visit our website to buy online.

Tel: 0131 2083333   www.Vicarious-Shop.com

Vicarious Shop

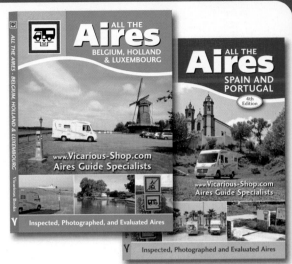

- 3034 Aires for France
- 449 Aires for Spain and Portugal
- 197 Aires for Holland
- 119 Aires for Belgium, plus 13 for Luxembourg
- Extensive LPG listings for every country

Sample Spain and Portugal entry. Entries for Belgium, Luxembourg and Holland follow the same format.

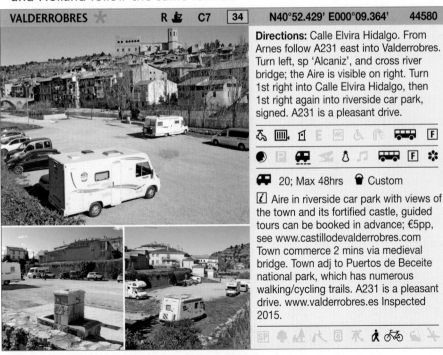

VALERROBRES R C7 34 N40°52.429' E000°09.364' 44580

Directions: Calle Elvira Hidalgo. From Arnes follow A231 east into Valderrobres. Turn left, sp 'Alcaniz', and cross river bridge; the Aire is visible on right. Turn 1st right into Calle Elvira Hidalgo, then 1st right again into riverside car park, signed. A231 is a pleasant drive.

20; Max 48hrs Custom

Aire in riverside car park with views of the town and its fortified castle, guided tours can be booked in advance; €5pp, see www.castillodevalderrobres.com Town commerce 2 mins via medieval bridge. Town adj to Puertos de Beceite national park, which has numerous walking/cycling trails. A231 is a pleasant drive. www.valderrobres.es Inspected 2015.

Harbour at Looe, Cornwall

Blackpool Sands, Devon

Vicarious Shop

These unique campsite guides show you all the sea view campsites around Scotland and Wales. All you have to do is choose where you want to go and be ready for a fantastic time as you explore some of the most diverse coastlines in the world.

If you love being by the sea, then these campsite guides are for you.

only **£7.99** each
inc UK P&P

To order, give us a call or visit our website to buy online.

0131 208 3333   www.Vicarious-Shop.com

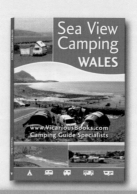

Going here?
Buy Sea View Camping Wales

N

17
18
19
14 11
12
20 16
21 7
8   5
6   1
3
9   4
10
13   2
22 Barnstaple
25 Taunton Yeovil
15
24 23
25
26 77
78
33 79
34 70 72
35 28 27
36 80 81
30 29
38 69
39 31 68
32 71
40 37 73
45 74
44 Plymouth 64 75 76
42 41 58 59 60
46 57 67
47 55 63
48 43 56
Falmouth 61 65
53 62 66
49 54
50 52
51

Bristol

Exeter

CONTENTS

Uphill Marine Centre

Uphill Wharf, Weston-super-Mare, Somerset,
BS23 4XR Tel: 01934 418617/07788 484098
http://uphillboatservices.co.uk

Although there are no sea views from this quirky boatyard and campsite, most pitches border a small saltwater lake; no swimming. The majority of grass pitches are level and have electric hook-up. 11 hardstanding pitches are located closest to the facilities and onsite cafe. Walk 400m along the River Axe to the links golf course and Weston-super-Mare's golden sandy beach. The Grand Pier is a pleasant 1.6 mile beachside walk. For panoramic views over the campsite and out to sea ascend the hill in Walborough Nature Reserve to the 12th century church and watch tower.

| NA 8.5 | NP 40 | 16 AMP | | |

Cafe, shop and slipway on site. Beach 400m. Pub 400m.

££££ 🐕 ♿ M CL CS ⓘ WiFi

Directions: Exit M5 at Junction 22. At roundabout turn onto A370 towards Weston-super-Mare. Follow A370 for 7 miles towards Weston-super-Mare, then turn left onto Uphill Road South, by the North Somerset sign. Drive for 400m, over a roundabout, then turn left, sp 'Uphill village & sands' with the campsite symbol. In 0.4 miles turn left again into Uphill Boat Centre. Enter site through the sea defence gate; during high spring tides the gate is closed for 1 hour either side of high tide.
GPS: N51°19.230' W002°59.066'
OS grid: 182 ST 315 584

All Year

Staple Farm *CL*

West Quantoxhead, Taunton, Somerset,
TA4 4EA Tel: 01984 632495

Situated on the western end of the Quantock Hills, this 1 acre sloping paddock is part of a traditional working farm. There are good views over the Somerset countryside to the Bristol Channel and Minehead, located at the foot of North Hill. The sand and shingle tidal estuary beaches are a long walk, or a short drive, away.

| NA 2 | NP 5 | | |

Pub and shop 400m.

££££ 🐕 ♿ M CL CS ⓘ WiFi

Directions: From Bridgwater head northwest on A39 towards Minehead. In West Quantoxhead, immediately past the Windmill Inn, turn left. Drive 230m uphill, going straight over the crossroads, and the farm is 50m on the right.

GPS: N51°09.950' W003°16.495'
OS grid: 181 ST 109 415

April - October

Home Farm Holiday Centre

St Audries Bay, Williton, Somerset,
TA4 4DP Tel: 01984 632487
www.homefarmholidaycentre.co.uk

Get away from it all at this tranquil, family site. The small level camping area offers views of St Audrie's Bay through trees and over 2 rows of privately owned statics. Some touring pitches can be rented for the season, altering pitch availability year to year, so advanced booking is recommended. The whole site has an old world charm to it, including the facilities. Just 100m away, the private beach is it a great place to cast a line, swim or hunt for fossils. Woodlands to one side provide space for walking, playing and exploring.

| NA | 45 | NP | 40 | 10/16 AMP |

Pub, cafe, beach and shop on site.

£££

Directions: Exit M5 at Junction 24 and take A38 (A39) towards Minehead for 17 miles to West Quantoxhead. After passing St Audrie's Service Station on the left, take the 1st right onto B3191, sp 'Blue Anchor Bay' and 'Doniford'. The site entrance is clearly signed on the right, 140m past the railway bridge. The site road has several traffic humps.

GPS: N51°10.444' W003°17.341'
OS grid: 181 ST 110 430

March - October

Helwell Bay Holidays

Watchet, Somerset, TA23 0UG
Tel: 01948 631781
www.helwellbay.com

This traditional site occupies a narrow clifftop strip right on the Bristol Channel, with views along the Somerset coastline and across to Wales. 6 touring pitches have views obstructed by hedges, but another 10 have good sea views. The best views are reserved for the single line of static caravans that are available for hire. The fossil rich beach is 0.25 mile's walk. Vintage and steam trains chug past immediately behind the site on the West Somerset Railway. From Watchet, 0.4 miles away, you can catch one of these trains to Minehead or Bishop's Lydeard near Taunton.

| NA | 6 | NP | 12 | 10 AMP |

Pub 100m. Slipway 0.5 miles at Watchet.

££££

Directions: Drive to Williton either on A358 from Taunton or on A39. At the bottom of Williton High Street turn left onto B3191, then turn right at the Masons Arms. Follow this road to the end and turn left. As you enter Watchet the sea will be on your right. Follow the road and turn left at the Helwell Bay Holidays sign.

GPS: N51°10.830' W003°19.402'
OS grid: 181 ST 077 432

March - October

Warren Bay Holiday Village

Watchet, Somerset, TA23 0JR
Tel: 01984 631460
www.warrenbayholidayvillage.co.uk

The site entrance, with reception on one side and a heated indoor pool on the other, does not seem to prepare you for the amazing journey through the park to the clifftop camping field. This sloping field is triangular with its longest side adjacent to the cliff. The higher and narrower you pitch, the better the view. Behind, 250 statics sit comfortably on terraces amongst native and exotic trees and shrubs. The facilities are very good. A steep path leads to the private stony and mudflat beach. Over 200 bird species have been seen on and around the site.

| NA | 28 | NP | 150 | 16 AMP | | |

| WC | | | | | | MG | MB |

Pub, shop, beach and slipway at Watchet.

££££ 🐕 †† Ⓜ CL CS ⓘ WiFi

Directions: 1.25 miles west of Watchet on B3191.

GPS: N51°10.657' W003°20.999'
OS grid: 181 ST 058 430

Easter - October

Warren Farm

Watchet, Somerset, TA23 0JP
Tel: 01984 631220

This campsite is as old as the hills. Well not quite, but it was established in 1928 and is part of a 260 acre farm. The site spreads over several fields, each area offering a different view and atmosphere but all having plenty of space. The site owners are charming and drive around the extensive site in the mornings, delivering papers and provisions. There are two toilet blocks and, though they are not state of the art, they are well maintained and immaculately kept.

| NA | 14 | NP | 100 | 0 AMP | | |

| WC | | | | | | MG | MB |

Pub, shop, beach and slipway 1.5 miles at Watchet.

££££ 🐕 †† Ⓜ CL CS ⓘ WiFi

Directions: 1.5 miles west of Watchet on B3191.

GPS: N51°10.718' W003°21.547'
OS grid: 181 ST 050 431

April - Mid October

Home Farm CS

Blue Anchor, Minehead, Somerset, TA24 6JS
Tel: 01984 640817
www.homefarmblueanchor.co.uk

Home Farm is a small working livestock farm adjacent to the sea, but is behind a sea wall and a road, so has no sea views. There is a huge tide in the Bristol Channel and the sand and pebble beach can be vast or nonexistent. This means the water is warm and shallow and there is good rock pooling. The campsite owners organise one of the best summer boot fairs in the country: Saturdays 2-5pm. Blue Anchor has two real ale pubs and the one onsite offers good food. The campsite has a pleasant tearoom and there is a seafront café. This is a member's only site, affiliated to the Camping and Caravanning Club, but you can join on arrival.

| NA | 3 | NP | 20 | ☠ 10 AMP | | |

Pub 100m. Restaurant on site. Shop and indoor pool on adjoining site. Slipway 150m.

£££**£** 🐕 ♦♦ Ⓜ CL CS ① WiFi

Directions: From Bridgwater head west on A39. Drive through Washford, then after 0.5 miles take the 1st right onto B3191, sp 'Blue Anchor', 'Old Cleeve' and 'Chapel Cleeve'. Drive to the end of the road, to the Blue Anchor pub, and turn left along the seafront. The farm entrance is 300m on the left and shares its entrance with the Smugglers Inn.

GPS: N51°10.953' W003°23.406'
OS grid: 181 ST 029 435

April - October

Hoburne Blue Anchor

Blue Anchor Bay, Nr Minehead, Somerset, TA24 6JT Tel: 01643 821360
www.hoburne.com/park-details/hoburne-blue-anchor

This family friendly holiday park is set in open fields adjacent to the sea, but most of the site is lower than the sea wall and there is no sea view from the touring field. Blue Anchor Bay offers an expansive sea view all the way to the tip of Wales on a clear day. The park has an indoor leisure pool, crazy golf, nature trail and outdoor adventure playground. The onsite convenience store also sells tackle and bait. Fishing from the sea wall is popular, and dogfish are often caught. The cliff walk to Watchet is lovely and you can catch a steam train back to Blue Anchor.

| NA | 13 | NP | 113 | ☠ 10 AMP | | |

Shop and indoor pool on site. Pub 100m. Slipway 300m

£££**£** 🐕 ♦♦ Ⓜ CL CS ① WiFi

Directions: From Bridgwater head west on A39. Drive through Washford, then after 0.5 miles take the 1st right onto B3191, sp 'Blue Anchor', 'Old Cleeve' and 'Chapel Cleeve'. Drive to the end of the road, to the Blue Anchor pub, and turn left along the seafront. The farm entrance is 500m on the left, clearly signed.

GPS: N51°10.940' W003°23.823'
OS grid: 181 ST 024 434

April - October

Minehead Camping and Caravanning Club Site `9`

Hill Road, North Hill, Minehead, Somerset,
TA24 5LB Tel: 01643 704138
www.campingandcaravanningclub.co.uk

This site is perched high above Minehead on North Hill, part of Exmoor National Park. Not every pitch has sea views, but the location is stunning. Many trees and shrubs have been cleared in recent years, which affords more of the pitches lovely views of the sea and across to Minehead. The facilities are not new, but are well kept. It is a long, but walkable 1.5 miles to the beach or Minehead, however walkers need only walk out of the gate to set foot on the moor and see the ponies.

| NA 3 | NP 60 | 16 AMP | | |

Pub, shop, beach and slipway at Minehead.

££££ 🐕 ♊ M CL CS ⓘ WiFi

Directions: From either direction on A39 drive to Minehead town centre, not the seafront. At Wellington Square, opposite HSBC bank, turn into the high street (The Parade). Take the 2nd left into Blenheim Road, then the next left into Martlet Road. Keep left at the church and follow a narrow, steep and twisting road for 1 mile. The site is on the right. No caravans allowed.

GPS: N51°12.834' W003°29.680'
OS grid: 181 SS 958 471

May - September

Napps Touring Holidays `10`

Old Coast Road, Berrynarbor, North Devon,
EX34 9SW Tel: 01271 882557
www.napps.co.uk

Delightfully located in an area of outstanding natural beauty, this is a really pleasant and quiet touring and tenting only site. The pitching areas are terraced into the hillside, providing increasingly beautiful views the higher you climb. There is an outdoor heated pool, a nice bar and grill, a well stocked shop and superb toilets. The sea and sandy beach are only 0.5 miles away, down 220 steps.

| NA 45 | NP 200 | 10 AMP | | |

Pub and shop on site. Broadlands Beach 200m. Beach and slipway 500m at Watermouth.

££££ 🐕 ♊ M CL CS ⓘ WiFi

Directions: 2 miles southwest of Combe Martin and 3 miles east of Ilfracombe on A399. The site owner advises that you avoid Barnstaple as it is often congested, and that you avoid the A39 coastal route from Minehead and Porlock as the road is narrow and extremely steep in parts.

GPS: N51°12.512' W004°03.863'
OS grid: 180 SS 559 479

March - October

Damage Barton

Mortehoe, Woolacombe, North Devon,
EX34 7EJ Tel: 01271 870502
www.damagebarton.co.uk

A site of two halves. One half is reserved for Caravan Club members only and the other half welcomes all campers. Just about every pitch has great sea views as far as the Welsh coast. Standards are high across the entire park. One toilet block is new and the other is due to be replaced for 2016. Watch the lambing at Easter on the 580 acre working farm or discover the beauty of the South West Coast Path or the Tarka Trail cycleway, which both run nearby. Lee Bay is 1.5 miles away, about 25 mins walk, but there is also a bus stop conveniently located at the campsite entrance.

| NA 16 | NP 150 | 10 AMP | | |

Shop on site. Pub 1.2 miles at Mortehoe. WiFi in shop courtyard only.

£££ 🐕 †† M CL CS (i) WiFi

Directions: From Barnstaple on A316 travel 10 miles towards Ilfracombe. At the Mullacott Cross roundabout turn left onto B3343 towards Woolacombe. In 1.7 miles turn right into Mortehoe Station Road, sp 'Mortehoe' and campsite name. The campsite entrance is 1 mile on the right, clearly signed.

GPS: N51°11.025' W004°11.312'
OS grid: 180 SS 471 451

Mid March - October

Sandaway Beach Holiday Park

Woodlands, Coombe Martin, North Devon,
EX24 9ST Tel: 01271 866766
www.johnfowlerholidays.com

From many of the holiday homes on this park there are excellent sea views, though no view is available from the small touring area. A modest tent area set amongst trees does have a nice view through a break in the trees, but the best views are enjoyed from the bar or as you explore the park. A 150m walk down a picturesque, stepped path brings you to Sandaway Beach, which is privately owned by the campsite.

| NA 20 | NP 20 | 16 AMP | | |

Beach and swimming pool on site. Pub, shop and slipway 1.5 miles at Watermouth Cove.

££££ 🐕 †† M CL CS (i) WiFi

Directions: The campsite is adjacent to A399 400m northwest of Combe Martin.

GPS: N51°12.377' W004°02.690'
OS grid: 180 SS 571 471

March - November

Sunnymead Farm 13

Mullacott, Ilfracombe, North Devon,
EX34 8NZ Tel: 01271 879845
www.sunnymead-farm.co.uk

This site offers some of the least expensive camping in the area, which is fair as it is not as well located as other local sites and has only a distant view of the sea across farmland. There are two level paddocks alongside the busy B3343, which cater for 5 tourers and plenty of tents. 10 electric hook-ups are available. There are two static caravans for hire and another acre of land is available for rallies. There is an onsite cafe and takeaway in high season, however at other times meals can be pre-ordered.

| NA | 1.5 | NP | 30 | 16 AMP | | |

Cafe and takeaway on site (high season). Pub 1 mile.

££££ 🐕 👫 M CL CS ⓘ WiFi

Directions: From Barnstaple on A316 travel 10 miles towards Ilfracombe. At the Mullacott Cross roundabout turn left onto B3343 towards Woolacombe. The site is approximately 0.5 miles on the right, just past the veterinary hospital, opposite the Highways Guest House.

GPS: N51°10.640' W004°08.793'
OS grid: 180 SS 499 442

Easter - October

Easewell Farm Holiday Park 14

Mortehoe Station Road, Woolacombe, Devon,
EX34 7EH Tel: 01271 871400
www.woolacombe.co.uk

Max 8.5m
Having driven around the beautifully kept 9-hole golf course, you arrive at the top of the campsite and can immediately appreciate the sea views that you will enjoy during your holiday. Laid out in terraces, the top most camping areas at the entrance command the best views. While not new, the facilities are plentiful and include a heated indoor pool, indoor bowls, snooker, golf, children's play area, arcade, restaurant and licensed club. There is also shared use of the facilities at the sister campsites: Twitchen House, Golden Coast and Woolacombe Bay.

| NA | 45 | NP | 300 | 16 AMP | | |

Pub, restaurant and swimming pool on site. Beach 5.5 miles at Ilfracombe.

££££ 🐕 👫 M CL CS ⓘ WiFi

Directions: From Barnstaple on A316 travel 10 miles towards Ilfracombe. At the Mullacott Cross roundabout turn left onto B3343 towards Woolacombe. In 1.7 miles turn right into Mortehoe Station Road, sp 'Mortehoe' and campsite name. Travel 1.5 miles and the campsite and golf course entrance is on the right, clearly signed.

GPS: N51°11.237' W004°12.012'
OS grid: 180 SS 462 455

March - October

Mullacott Farm CS

Ilfracombe, North Devon, EX34 8NA
Tel: 01271 866877
www.mullacottfarm.co.uk

This rustic, family-friendly farm site has a relaxed and noncommercial feel. The hilly camping field offers no sea views. From other areas there are distant sea views over countryside. Non member tent campers are welcome. Reception sells fresh eggs and some farm produce, including wool and local meat boxes. Navigate Walker's Woods on a quad bike, or book a beach gallop with the horse riding school, both adjacent. Tunnels Beaches, with its hand carved tunnels and tidal Victorian bathing pool, is 2 miles at Ilfracombe.

NA	8	NP	20	🎯 16 AMP		

WC						MG	MB

Pub and swimming pool 400m at Ilfracombe. Beach 2 miles at Ilfracombe or 4 miles at Woolacombe.

£££ 🐕 †† M CL CS ⓘ WiFi

Directions: From Barnstaple on A316 travel to Ilfracombe. Pass over the crossroads where B3343 bisects A361 and the site is 0.5 miles on the left. Large units accepted, but must phone in advance.

GPS: N51°11.139' W004°07.729'
OS grid: 180 SS 514 453

Easter - Mid October

North Morte Farm
Caravan and Camping Park

Mortehoe, Woolacombe, North Devon,
EX34 7EG Tel: 01271 870381
www.northmortefarm.co.uk

Camping here is as it should be, wild but civilised. The sea views are absolutely stunning and the stargazing is exceptional. The site entrance is just off Mortehoe village centre, convenient to shops and restaurants. The camping fields are in the moors, but are all well manicured to enable comfortable camping. There are modern toilet blocks, serviced touring pitches, and static caravans for hire.

NA	25	NP	175	🎯 16 AMP		

WC						MG	MB

Pub 400m at Mortehoe. Beach 1 mile.

£££ 🐕 †† M CL CS ⓘ WiFi

Directions: From Barnstaple on A316 travel 10 miles towards Ilfracombe. At the Mullacott Cross roundabout turn left onto B3343 towards Woolacombe. In 1.7 miles turn right into Mortehoe Station Road, sp 'Mortehoe' and campsite name. Travel 1.9 miles to Mortehoe and turn right into North Morte Road by The Smugglers Rest. The site is 400m on the left.

VisitEngland
★★★★
HOLIDAY, TOURING & CAMPING PARK

GPS: N51°11.301' W004°12.216'
OS grid: 180 SS 461 457

Easter - October

Europa Park

Beach Road, Woolacombe, Devon,
EX34 7AN Tel: 01271 871425
www.europapark.co.uk

Europa Park is a lively, vibrant site with a great atmosphere and an awesome sea view towards Lundy that can be seen from most of the site. This is probably the only campsite in the county that actively encourages stag and hen parties, thus it has separate family, adults only and party fields and several different toilet blocks. On site there is a cafe, indoor pool, sauna, games room, off licence and late night bar complete with rodeo bull. Activity packages can be arranged through H2Outdoor. Woolacombe village and beach are 1.2 miles away.

| NA | 16 | NP | 300 | 16 AMP | | |

| WC | | | | | | MG | MB |

Indoor swimming pool, pub, restaurant and takeaway on site. Beach 1.2 miles at Woolacombe.

££££ M CL CS (i) WiFi

Directions: From Barnstaple on A316 travel 10 miles towards Ilfracombe. At the Mullacott Cross roundabout turn left onto B3343 towards Woolacombe. The site entrance is 2.7 miles on the right beside a fuel station and Spar, approximately 1 mile from Woolacombe.

GPS: N51°10.273' W004°11.006'
OS grid: 180 SS 473 437

All Year

Warcombe Farm Camping Park

Station Road, Mortehoe, North Devon,
EX34 7EJ Tel: 01271 870690
www.warcombefarm.co.uk

Max 9.5m

This charming, landscaped site gently slopes towards the sea and is split in two by the carp fishing lake. The top half has the best sea views stretching across the Bristol Channel. The lower part of the park is separated into small hedged areas and the sea can be glimpsed over the Devon hedge from the pitches closest to the sea. The toilet blocks offer exceptional quality, including underfloor heating. There are good facilities for dogs and access to the South West Coast Path from the top of the site. Woolacombe Bay is 1.5 miles via footpath.

| NA | 19 | NP | 260 | 16 AMP | | |

| WC | | | | | | MG | MB |

Pub, shop, beach and slipway 1.5 miles at Woolacombe Bay.

££££ M CL CS (i) WiFi

Directions: From Barnstaple on A316 travel 10 miles towards Ilfracombe. At the Mullacott Cross roundabout turn left onto B3343 towards Woolacombe. In 1.7 miles turn right into Mortehoe Station Road, sp 'Mortehoe' and campsite name. Travel 0.6 miles and the campsite is on the right, clearly signed.

GPS: N51°10.746' W004°10.868'
OS grid: 180 SS 478 422

March - October

Sandy Lane, Woolacombe, Devon,
EX34 7AH Tel: 01271 870221
www.woolacombe.co.uk

Moor Lane, Croyde Bay, Devon, EX33 1NZ
Tel: 07581 024348
www.oceanpitch.co.uk

© Matt Lenster

Max 6m

This is a large, terraced, family park with some excellent sea views. Unfortunately the majority of the touring pitches are at the far end of the site with limited sea views. There are a wide range of facilities on offer, including indoor pool, adventure golf, tennis and bowls as well as relaxation at Romano Spa and a lively nightlife. There is a bus, and a footpath, to the beach and a bus to the sister sites: Twitchen House, Golden Coast and Easewell Farm, whose facilities campers can also enjoy.

The new owners have not only changed the site's name from Mitchum's Campsite, they have also made it trendy and appealing for surfers. Every pitch has a sea view, although impeded by hedges in some areas. The two glamping tents at the top of the site enjoy the best views out across Croyde Bay. The sandy beach and surf are just 45m away. Surfing and body boarding equipment can be hired on site. You can stay up late every night, at least until 12:30am when quiet time begins. With this in mind, the site welcomes families with children over 5 years old.

| NA 15 | NP 171 | 16 AMP | | |

| WC | | | | | MG | MB |

Pub, shop and swimming pool on site. Beach 1 mile. Slipway 7 miles at Ilfracombe.

| NA 1 | NP 40 | 0 AMP | | |

| WC | | | | | MG | MB |

Pub, shop, children's play area, swimming pool and laundry at Park Dean Ruda.

££££ 🐕 ††† M CL CS (i) WiFi

£££ 🐕 ††† M CL CS (i) WiFi

Directions: From Barnstaple on A316 travel 10 miles towards Ilfracombe. At the Mullacott Cross roundabout turn left onto B3343 towards Woolacombe. In 1.7 miles turn right into Mortehoe Station Road, sp 'Mortehoe' and campsite name. Travel 0.7 miles and turn left into Sandy Lane, clearly signed, and the site is in 400m.

VisitEngland
★★★★
HOLIDAY, TOURING & CAMPING PARK

Directions: From Braunton on B3231 travel to Croyde. In Croyde village turn left onto Jones's Hill, sp 'Croyde Beach', then turn left onto Moor Lane, sp 'Croyde Beach' with the campsite symbol. The campsite is 0.6 miles on the right.

GPS: N51°10.625' W004°11.468'
OS grid: 180 SS 469 435

GPS: N51°08.066' W004°14.294'
OS grid: 180 SS 435 397

Easter - October

Mid June - August

Putsborough Sands

Putsborough, Georgeham, Nr Braunton,
North Devon, EX33 1LB Tel: 01271 890230
www.putsborough.com

Just feet from the sand, this 2 acre site directly overlooks an enormous, sandy surfing beach. The touring caravan pitches are in a sheltered area, with some gently sloping and terraced parts. Campervans may be able to park at the top of the car park for a fee and on a first come, first served basis, but there is no other motorhome area or any camping for tents. The facilities are top of the line, modern and immaculately kept. This is an absolutely perfect site for caravanners to have a beach holiday, especially if you like to surf, sail or windsurf.

| NA 2 | NP 25 | 16 AMP | | |

Campervan users have no access to the showers.

££££ M CL CS WiFi

Directions: The site owners recommend a one-way system, so approaching campers should come from Braunton on B3231, travel through Croyde and continue onto Georgeham. Then turn left following sp 'Putsborough' and 'Sands'. All the roads to the site are narrow, so avoid travelling to the site between 4-6pm when people are leaving the beach and at 9am and 3pm during school terms.

GPS: N51°08.614' W004°13.198'
OS grid: 180 SS 448 405

Easter - September

Twitchen House

Morehoe, Woolacombe, Devon, EX34 7ES
Tel: 01271 970848
www.woolacombe.com

Max 8m

This large site has more than enough to keep the whole family occupied during your stay. There are views of the sea from the upper touring field, and you can book a sea view pitch, but the statics have the best views. The onsite facilities are extensive and campers also have access to all the sister sites' facilities. There are buses between sites and a footpath to Woolacombe Bay Holiday Village. Woolacombe village and beach are 1.8 miles away along the South West Coast Path.

| NA 60 | NP 333 | 16 AMP | | |

Shop, swimming pool, arcade and cinema on site. Beach 2 miles.

££££ M CL CS WiFi

Directions: From Barnstaple on A316 travel 10 miles towards Ilfracombe. At the Mullacott Cross roundabout turn left onto B3343 towards Woolacombe. In 1.7 miles turn right into Mortehoe Station Road, sp 'Mortehoe' and campsite name. Travel 1.4 miles and the site entrance is on the left, clearly signed.

GPS: N51°10.985' W004°11.844'
OS grid: 180 SS 465 448

Easter - October

Wooda Farm Holiday Park

Poughill, Bude, Cornwall, EX23 9HJ
Tel:01288 352069
www.wooda.co.uk

Max 10m

This five-star, family run campsite has lovely distant sea views from the majority of pitches. Although the site is large, you can feel the effort that is put into ensuring everything is tip top. Most of the 40-acre site is available for tenters and tourers who have a choice of grass, hardstanding or fully serviced pitches. Also available are 55 statics, 2 cottages and Bessie the 1950s caravan. The well maintained facilities are plentiful and staff are more than happy to meet specific requests or create activities for children or families. Bude town and the beach are 1.5 miles away.

NA	40	NP	220	16 AMP		

Pub/restaurant, takeaway and shop on site. Beach and slipway 1.5 miles at Bude.

££££ 🐕 †† M CL CS ⓘ WiFi

Directions: From Wadebridge on A39 travel north towards Bude. On the outskirts of Stratton turn left following sp to 'Poughill' and 'Combe valley'. The site is on the right after 0.75 mile.

VisitEngland
★★★★★
HOLIDAY, TOURING & CAMPING PARK

GPS: N50°50.623' W004°31.070'
OS grid: 190 SS 229 079

Easter - October

Ivyleaf *CL*

Ivyleaf Farm, Stratton, Bude, Cornwall, EX23 9LD Tel: 01288 321592
www.ivyleafgolf.com

This *CL* is way above par. There are 5 hardstanding, serviced bays in a hedged corner overlooking the golf course. The views stretch across countryside to the sea in the distance. Being part of, and adjacent to, a golf course, campers have use of the toilets, showers and washing machines. Weekly golf passes are available and archery and paintball are possible. Visitors must book in at reception on arrival. Advanced booking is recommended.

NA	1	NP	5	16 AMP		

Pub and shop 1.5 miles at Poughill. Beach and slipway 3.5 miles at Bude.

££££ 🐕 †† M CL CS ⓘ WiFi

Directions: Located halfway between Kilkhampton and Stratton. From Stratton travel 1 mile north and turn right, sp 'Ivy Leaf Golf Course'. Drive 0.5 miles up this road and the site is on the left, clearly signed.

GPS: N50°51.129' W004°30.260'
OS grid: 190 SS 241 085

All Year

Penhalt Farm Holiday Park

Widemouth Bay, Poundstock, Bude,
Cornwall EX23 0DG Tel: 01288 361210
www.penhaltfarm.co.uk

Penhalt sits high on the coastal downs, 1.3 miles south of Widemouth Bay. Every pitch offers commanding views of the magnificent Atlantic coastline and the beautiful surrounding countryside. This site would be the editor's choice if visiting Widemouth Bay, having a preference for open spaces and simple sites. There is a 6-berth caravan, a 3-bedroom farmhouse flat and a 3-bedroom bungalow all available for hire. Widemouth Bay is a popular sandy beach good for surfing and swimming. The South West Coast Path can be picked up 0.5 miles from the site.

| NA 8 | NP 40+ | 10 AMP | | |

Shop on site. Beach 0.5 miles downhill.

£££

Directions: From Bude on A39 take the 2nd turning to Widemouth, sp 'Widemouth Bay Caravan Park'. Follow this road until just past the Widemouth Manor Hotel. Turn left, sp 'Widemouth Bay' and 'Penhalt Farm'. Penhalt Farm is on the left in 1 mile, clearly signed.

VisitEngland
★★★
TOURING &
CAMPING PARK

GPS: N50°46.635' W004°33.960'
OS grid: 190 SS 194 003

April - October

Sandymouth Holiday Home Park

Stibb, Nr Bude, Cornwall, EX23 9HW
Tel: 08442 729530
www.sandymouthbay.co.uk

This site affords one of the best sea views in the west. From the touring pitches and 10 acre camping field there are awesome panoramic views of both coast and countryside. This is a big family park with lots of quality accommodation and excellent facilities, including an indoor swimming pool, gym and the Black Pearl pirate ship play area. However, despite the size of the park, due to the location of the camping area, you feel like you are there on your own. The beach is 0.5 miles downhill (uphill on the way back!), and the sand is beyond a maze of stones and boulders.

| NA 24 | NP 50 | 10 AMP | | |

Bar, cafe and shop on site. Pub, shop and slipway 400m at Bude.

£££

Directions: South of Kirkhampton turn off A39, sp 'Sandymouth'. Follow the road for 1 mile and, after the village of Stibb, turn left, sp 'Sandymouth Holiday Park' and 'Sandymouth Bay National Trust'. The site is 450m on the left.

GPS: N50°52.012' W004°32.249'
OS grid: 190 SS 217 107

March - October

Bude Camping and Caravanning Club Site | 27

Gillards Moor, St Gennys, Bude, Cornwall, EX23 0BG Tel: 01840 230650
www.campingandcaravanningclub.co.uk

Located 8 miles from Bude and 3 miles from the sea, the views from this friendly site are distant at best. Nevertheless, the countryside views are lovely and the proximity to the Atlantic highway makes it easy to go sightseeing. However, road noise is present and walking anywhere involves a stretch of the busy A39. The site and facilities are kept well, although not new. Pitches are a mixture of grass, gravel and hardstanding. The nearest sandy beach and access to the South West Coast Path are at Crackington Haven, 3.7 miles away.

| NA | 8.5 | NP | 100 | 16 AMP |

Pub 1 mile at St Gennys. Beach 3.7 miles at Crackington Haven. Slipway 5 miles at Wigmouth Bay. Swimming pool 8 miles at Bude.

£££ 🐕 ♦♦ M CL CS ⓘ WiFi

Directions: From Wadebridge on A39 travel north towards Bude. This site is on the left in a lay-by 8 miles from Bude.

GPS: N50°43.146' W004°35.076'
OS grid: 190 SX 176 943

April - October

Widemouth Bay Caravan Park | 28

Poundstock, Bude, Cornwall, EX23 0DF
Tel: 01288 361208
www.johnfowlerholidays.com

This park is big and lively with 50 acres to explore and an abundance of facilities and amenities. The very popular, mostly sloping camping area is well away from the main park at the top of the hill. From many of the pitches the sea can be seen, but the countryside views are better. Sandy Widemouth Bay is 0.75 miles downhill and is very popular because of the good bathing and wonderful surfing.

| NA | 50 | NP | 120 | 16 AMP |

££££ 🐕 ♦♦ M CL CS ⓘ WiFi

Directions: From Bude travel 3 miles south on A39 and take the 2nd turning, sp 'Widemouth Bay'. Travel 0.9 miles and turn left adjacent to Widemouth Manor Hotel, sp for campsite. The site entrance is 300m on the left. Turn left into the site road and drive up to reception. Drivers of large vehicles must phone in advance.

GPS: N50°46.594' W004°33.153'
OS grid: 190 SS 198 008

March - October

Trewethett Farm Caravan Club Site   **29**

Trethevy, Tintagel, PL34 0BQ
Tel: 01840 770222
www.caravanclub.co.uk

Perched directly on the Cornish cliffs, this immaculately kept site offers fantastic luxury and there are breathtaking sea views from all areas of the site. The serviced, level touring pitches benefit from being arranged on several terraces and there is a separate camping field. The South West Coast Path borders the site and there are spectacular clifftop walks to be enjoyed.

| NA 15 | NP 146 | 16 AMP | | |

Pub and slipway at Boscastle. Shop at Tintagel.

£££**£** WiFi

Directions: From Tintagel on B3263 travel towards Boscastle. In 1.6 miles turn left, clearly signed, and follow road to site.

GPS: N50°40.439' W004°43.606'
OS grid: 200 SX 074 897

March - November

Headland Caravan Park   **30**

Atlantic Road, Tintagel, Cornwall, PL34 0DE
Tel: 01840 770239
www.headlandcaravanpark.co.uk

Location, Location, Location! Tintagel, just outside the gate, boasts many pubs, restaurants, tearooms, local shops and attractions. There are partial sea views from some areas on this reasonably large, mostly level site. The best sea views can be seen from Tintagel Castle, the legendary birthplace of King Arthur, a short 0.7 mile walk away. This campsite makes a great rest stop for walkers following the South West Coast Path, or users of large motorhomes or campers without additional means of transport.

| NA 5 | NP 20 | 16 AMP | | |

Slipway at Boscastle.

£££**£** WiFi

Directions: Follow B3263 to Tintagel. Drive straight through village following sp 'Headland' and 'Caravan Park'. The site is on the right before the headland.

GPS: N50°39.995' W004°45.084'
OS grid: 200 SX 055 887

Easter - October

Pennycrocker Farm

Boscastle, Cornwall, PL35 0BY
Tel: 07967 605392
www.pennycrocker.com

Spacious and level, this clifftop site is part of a working farm in an absolutely beautiful setting. There are good sea views and wonderful views over 15 miles of countryside to Padstow and beyond. Access to the sea is about a 10 mins drive away and from the coast path you can walk to Cornwall's highest cliffs. There are also onsite fishing lakes, which are stocked with carp and tench.

| NA | 6 | NP | 40 | 16 AMP | | |

Directions: From Bude on A39 travel south towards Wadebridge. Pass Wainhouse Corner, then in 1.5 miles turn onto B3263, sp 'Boscastle'. Travel 2.75 miles and turn right off B3263, sp 'Lower Pennycrocker Camping'. Follow campsite signs for 0.5 miles down the narrow, single track road (there are some passing areas) and the site is on the left, clearly signed.

GPS: N50°42.278' W004°39.386'
OS grid: 190 SX 125 927

Easter - October

Chapel Farm *CL*

Edmonton, Wadebridge, Cornwall, PL27 7JA
Tel: 01208 816140
www.caravanclub.co.uk

Tucked away in a rural location, this informal, 5 pitch site is level at the top before sloping away. There are fine countryside views leading on over the estuary, out to sea and across to Padstow. Visitors are trusted to pay in an honesty box. The local country pub is very attractive with an excellent reputation for food, and is only 2 mins walk away.

| NA | 1 | NP | 5 | 0 AMP | | |

Pub 100m. Shop adjacent to A39.

Directions: From Wadebridge on A39 travel south towards Truro. Go straight over the Shell roundabout, then turn right in 200m, sp 'Edmonton'. Follow the lane for 0.5 miles and pass The Quarryman pub on the right. When the road divides, enter the site through the gate that divides both lanes.

GPS: N50°31.131' W004°52.468'
OS grid: 200 SW 963 728

April - September

33	34
Higher Harlyn Park	**Atlantic View Camping and Touring**

St Merryn, Padstow, Cornwall, PL28 8SG Tel: 01841 520022 www.higherharlynpark.co.uk	Trevemedar Farm, St Eval, Wadebridge, Cornwall, PL27 7UT Tel: 01841 520431

This is a large site which is mostly occupied with seasonal statics. Only 8 touring pitches have electric and only another 20 or so have possible sea views, but both electric and views can be booked. The top field is reserved for touring and extra fields can be opened up in summer, so pitches are never overcrowded. The toilet block was updated in 2014 and is clean and modern. There is a heated swimming pool and shop on site. Constantine Bay is only 1 mile away and Padstow with all its amenities is only 3.5 miles away.

This large, mostly level grass site has fabulous sea views from every pitch. You cannot book, but there is an overflow field used during busy periods. The toilet block is basic, but the stunning views across Porthcothan Bay more than make up for them. Follow the South West Coast Path for 0.75 miles to the sandy, surfing beach and small village at Porthcothan.

NA 120	NP 100+	16 AMP		NA 16	NP 90	0 AMP	
WC			MG	WC			

Restaurant, bars (adults only and family) and swimming pool on site. Beach 1 mile.

Shop 0.5 miles in Porthcothan. Pub and swimming pool 2 miles at St Merryn. Slipway 6 miles at Padstow.

££££ WiFi

££££

Directions: From Wadebridge on A39 travel south towards Truro. In 5 miles turn right at the roundabout onto B3274, sp 'Padstow'. In 3 miles turn left at the crossroads to St Merryn, then travel 3 more miles to St Merryn centre. At the crossroads go straight over and the site is on the left in 0.5 miles, clearly signed.

Directions: From Padstow on B3276 head southwest towards Newquay. Go through St Merryn and Porth Cothan. The site is on the right 0.5 miles south of Porth Cothan, clearly signed.

GPS: N50°31.836' W004°59.752'
OS grid: 200 SW 877 744

GPS: N50°30.053' W005°01.461'
OS grid: 200 SW 854 714

Easter - October	**April - October**

Left listing

This site is meticulously managed which creates a unique atmosphere. The pitches, most with a sea view, are laid out around the edge of two large fields, leaving plenty of space for well behaved children to play. There is an additional dog walking field which offers fantastic views. The owners also run a gluten free bakery and cafe on site. The dog-friendly, lifeguarded beach at Treyarnon Bay is only a few hundred metres, but there is no vehicle access. The coast path runs close by and the site is surrounded by bird protection areas which are great for bird watching.

| NA 15 | NP 63 | 10 AMP | | |

| WC | | | | | | MG | MB |

Cafe on site. Pub 1 mile. Shop, beach and slipway at Padstow.

££££

Directions: From Padstow on B3276 head southwest towards Newquay. Travel through St Merryn, then in 0.8 miles take the 3rd right, sp 'Treyarnon' and 'Trethias' with the campsite symbol. Follow the campsite signs for 0.75 miles to reception by the farm in the village, which is a significant distance from the campsite. Maximum 8.5m (28ft) - if you're brave enough.

VisitEngland
★★★★
TOURING & CAMPING PARK

GPS: N50°31.365' W005°01.425'
OS grid: 200 SW 856 733

April - September

Right listing

Adjacent to a small, but popular, sandy beach (pictured), this is a traditional camping and static caravan site. There are several areas with sea views as you move through the park. The 21 electric hook-up pitches must be booked Saturday-Saturday. The camping field has clean, mobile toilet blocks nearby, but is set furthest from the beach and shower block. Site visitors are charged to use the showers, which are also available to beach visitors. Disabled toilet facilities are planned for 2016. The beach is a great place for kids and has a lifeguard in attendance. Dogs not allowed in high season.

| NA 10 | NP 60 | 10 AMP | | |

| WC | | | | | | MG | MB |

££££

Directions: From Padstow on B3276 head southwest towards Newquay. Travel through St Merryn, then in 0.8 miles take the 3rd right, sp 'Treyarnon' and 'Trethias' with the campsite symbol. Follow sp 'Treyarnon Bay' for 1 mile. The site entrance is in the beach car park. Large motorhomes are accepted, but access is difficult down the Cornish lanes.

enjoyEngland.com
★★★★
SELF CATERING

GPS: N50°31.660' W005°01.224'
OS grid: 200 SW 858 741

April - September

Watergate Bay Touring Park

Newquay, Cornwall, TR8 4AD
Tel: 01637 860387
www.watergatebaytouringpark.co.uk

Max 11.5m

This large, family site is only 200m from the sea, but the only views are from the outer reaches of the park. The pitches are all level grass, with some areas more densely packed than others. The swimming pool was refurbished in 2015 with a rollover canopy, so you can swim whatever the weather. There is nightly entertainment in the clubhouse bar and a kids' club to keep the little ones entertained. Just 0.5 miles from the site lie long stretches of beautiful sandy beach and numerous beachfront commerce to enjoy.

| NA 25 | NP 270 | ☠ 10/16 AMP | | |

| WC | ♿WC | 🚿 | 🛁 | 🚾 | ⬛ | MG | MB |

Pub, cafe, shop and swimming pool on site. Beach 0.5 miles. Slipway 4 miles at Newquay.

£££ 🐕 ♂♀ M CL CS ⓘ WiFi

Directions: From Bodmin on A30 travel southwest towards Redruth. In 19 miles exit onto A39 and follow sp 'Airport'. In 2.6 miles turn left at the 2nd roundabout onto A3059, sp 'Airport'. In 1.5 miles turn right, sp 'Airport'. After 1.5 miles turn left at the T-junction onto B327, sp 'Newquay', 'Porth' and 'Tregurrian'. The site is on the right in 0.5 miles.

VisitEngland
★★★★
HOLIDAY, TOURING & CAMPING PARK

GPS: N50°26.884' W005°01.610'
OS grid: 200 SW 851 655

March - October

Tregurrian Camping and Caravanning Club Site

Tregurrian, Nr Newquay, Cornwall, TR8 4AE Tel: 01637 860448
www.campingandcaravanningclub.co.uk

© Camping and Caravanning Club

Max 9m

One side of the site offers views across Watergate Bay and the other enjoys views across the wild Atlantic, although hedges obstruct views from some areas. The camping area is in a spacious field bordered with hedges and some pitches offer distant views of the sea. Facilities are up to the normal Camping and Caravanning Club standards. It's just 0.75 miles via a footpath to the glorious sandy beach at Watergate Bay, which is a haven for water sport lovers.

| NA 0.6 | NP 90 | ☠ 16 AMP | | |

| WC | ♿WC | 🚿 | 🛁 | 🚾 | ⬛ | MG | MB |

Beach 0.5 miles. Slipway and swimming pool 3 miles at Newquay.

££££ 🐕 ♂♀ M CL CS ⓘ WiFi

Directions: From St Columb Major on A39 turn onto A3059 towards Newquay, sp 'Airport'. In 1 mile turn right, sp 'Watermouth Bay' and 'Airport'. At T-Junction in 2.8 miles turn left onto B3276 towards Newquay. In 0.5 miles turn right, sp 'Tregurrian Campsite'. The site is 200m on the right.

GPS: N50°26.938' W005°01.850'
OS grid: 200 SW 847 654

April - October

Trevean Caravan and Camping Park `39`

Trevean Lane, St Merrryn, Padstow, Cornwall, PL28 8PR Tel: 01841 520772
www.treveancaravanandcamping.net

This is a very pleasant, small family run campsite on a working farm. From a few pitches there is a distant view of the sea over countryside. The layout and small number of pitches gives a cosy, friendly feel to the campsite. The village of St Merryn is about 1 mile away, as are the golden sands of Porthcothan, Treyarnon and Constantine bays.

| NA 6.5 | NP 71 | 16 AMP | | |

Pub and shop 1 mile at St Merryn/Porthcothan.

££££ 🐕 ♈ M CL CS ⓘ WiFi

Directions: From Padstow on B3276 travel southwest towards Newquay. Go through St Merryn, then in 1 mile turn left, sp 'Trevean 1 mile' with the campsite symbol. Despite the sign, the site is 0.5 miles on the right, clearly signed.

VisitEngland
★★★★
HOLIDAY, TOURING & CAMPING PARK

GPS: N50°30.766' W004°59.809'
OS grid: 200 SW 874 724

April - October

Beacon Cottage Farm Touring Park `40`

Beacon Drive, St Agnes, Cornwall, TR5 0NU
Tel: 01872 552347 / 07879 413862
www.beaconcottagefarmholidays.co.uk

As you enter the site, you pass by beautifully kept stone farm buildings, now used by the campsite, that make up part of this traditional, working Cornish family farm. There are some very secluded and cosy pitching spots (70 individually numbered), but the two main camping fields give excellent cliff and sea views as far as St Ives. This is a family friendly site located on the South West Coast Path, with the captivating remains of Wheal Coates tin mine just 200m away. Walkers welcome.

| NA 5 | NP 65 | 10 AMP | | |

Beach 0.5 miles. Pub and shop 1.5 miles in St Agnes.

£££ 🐕 ♈ M CL CS ⓘ WiFi

Directions: At the Chiverton roundabout on A30 turn right onto B3277, sp 'St Agnes'. In 3 miles, past Presingoll Barns, turn left at the mini roundabout, sp 'Chapel Porth'. In 4 miles turn left, sp 'Beacon Cottage Farm' with the campsite symbol. Follow these signs to the site, approximately 1 mile. Narrow with some passing areas.

VisitEngland
★★★★
TOURING & CAMPING PARK

GPS: N50°18.379' W005°13.585'
OS grid: 203 SW 703 501

March - October

Trevellas Manor Farm

Crosscombe, St Agnes, Cornwall,
TR5 0XP Tel: 01872 552238
www.trevellasmanorfarmcampsite.co.uk

Simply perfect and perfectly simple, this camping field gently slopes towards the wonderful sea view and the surrounding rolling countryside is dotted with bygone tin mines. St Agnes, about 2 miles away, has local commerce and restaurants and the beach is a 1 mile downhill walk away. The simple facilities, located by the farmhouse, are opposite the entrance to camping field.

| NA 6 | NP 60 | 16 AMP | | |

| WC | | | | | | MG | MB |

Beach 0.75 miles or 1 mile. Pub and shop 2 miles at St Agnes.

££££ M CL CS i WiFi

Directions: From St Agnes travel 1 mile towards Perranporth on B3285, then turn left, sp 'Cross Combe'. Do not take the 'Airport' or 'School' turning. Follow the road for 1.2 miles down a narrow lane, with some passing areas, and the campsite is on the left.

GPS: N50°19.287' W005°11.179'
OS grid: 203 SW 731 517

Easter - October

St Agnes Beacon Caravan Club Site

Beacon Drive, St Agnes, Cornwall, TR5 0NU
Tel: 01872 552543
www.caravanclub.co.uk

Max 9m
Old quarries seem to naturally convert into great campsites, and this site certainly benefits from its long lost industrial past. Situated at the foot of the Beacon, there are good views of the Cornish coastline. Much of the site is gently sloping and arranged on several levels, partly sheltered by gorse-topped banking. There is no toilet block, but high standards are maintained across the site, which has the usual club feel.

| NA 6 | NP 112 | 16 AMP | | |

| WC | | | | | O | MG | MB |

Beach 1.3 miles and pub and shop 2 miles at St Agnes.

££££ M CL CS i WiFi

Directions: The site is adjacent to Beacon Cottage Farm. At the Chiverton roundabout on A30 take B3277 to St Agnes. Turn left as you enter St Agnes. In 1.25 miles, over the crossroads, fork right into Beacon Drive. The site is the 2nd tarmac driveway on the right.

GPS: N50°18.448' W005°13.534'
OS grid: 203 SW 705 502

March - October

---

www.Vicarious-Shop.com

St Ives Bay Holiday Park

73 Loggans Road, Upton Towans, Hayle,
Cornwall, TR27 5BH Tel: 01736 752274
www.stivesbay.co.uk

© Chris Harvey

This large site is less than 500m from the beach. There are a mix of statics, chalets, camping pods and touring pitches, 24 of which have good sea views. The pitches are nestled amongst the sand dunes and are quite close together, but all campers have access to the 3-mile long sandy beach, 0.75 miles away down some steps. There are plenty of activities available on site, including crazy golf, an arcade and an adventure playground. Or you can relax with a refreshment in the bistro or at one of the onsite pubs and enjoy views over St Ives Bay.

| NA | 90 | NP | 258 | ☠ 16 AMP | | |

| WC | ♿ | ⛲ | 🛁 | 🚿 | ⭕ | MG | MB |

Pub, shop and swimming pool on site.
Slipway 1 mile at Hayle.

££££ 🐕 ♂♀ Ⓜ CL CS ⓘ WiFi

Directions: From Cambourne travel southwest on A30 until Loggans Moor roundabout. Take the 3rd exit towards Hayle onto B3301, then at the double mini roundabout turn right onto B3301. In 1 mile the site is clearly signed on the left.

GPS: N50°12.146' W005°23.939'
OS grid: 203 SW 571 394

April - September

Beachside Holiday Park

Hayle, Cornwall, TR27 5AW
Tel: 01736 753080
www.beachside.co.uk

Nestled amongst hundreds of acres of sand dunes, this unique campsite occupies 20 acres. Some pitching areas are gently sloping and all are spread through an amazing complex of sand dunes that any child would love to play within. Not all the pitches have views, but from some you can see the sea stretching to St Ives. There is plenty to explore and there is direct access to an enormous, quiet sandy beach via a walkway leading through the dunes. Closest to the sea, there is a small complex of retro holiday chalets for hire.

| NA | 8 | NP | 70 | ☠ 16 AMP | | |

| WC | ♿ | ⛲ | 🚿 | ⭕ | MG | MB |

££££ 🐕 ♂♀ Ⓜ CL CS ⓘ WiFi

Directions: Exit A30 at the large roundabout north of Hayle (McDonald's and Next) and take the road into Hayle, sp 'Hayle B3301/Helston B3302'. After 0.5 miles turn right by the putting green, sp 'The Towans', 'Phillack' and 'Beaches' and signed for the campsite. Follow the brown tourist signs to the site.

VisitEngland
★★★★
HOLIDAY, TOURING & CAMPING PARK

GPS: N50°12.132' W005°24.903'
OS grid: 203 SW 564 389

Easter - October

Ayr Holiday Park

St Ives, Cornwall, TR26 1EJ
Tel: 01736 795855
www.ayrholidaypark.co.uk

This campsite is conveniently located in the suburbs high above St Ives with direct access to the South West Coast Path. The elevated position enables excellent views across St Ives bay from most touring pitches and static caravans. During the day you can watch the surfers and swimmers, at night the illuminations set the scene. St Ives harbour is 0.5 miles downhill walk away; thankfully you can catch a bus back. The campsite facilities are exceptionally good and there are local shops and pubs close by. Unsurprisingly, this is a popular site.

| NA 10 | NP 68 | 16 AMP |

Pub, shop, beach and slipway 0.5 miles at St Ives.

££££

Directions: Exit A30 for St Ives. In 350m turn left at 2nd mini roundabout following signs to St Ives for heavy vehicles. In 3 miles turn right at T-Junction onto B3311. In 1 mile turn right at T-Junction onto B3306 towards St Ives. In 700m at 1st of 2 mini roundabouts turn left onto Carnellis Road, sp 'Ayr' with campsite symbol and 'Porthmeor Beach'. Follow road for 800m through a housing estate. Park entrance on left after sharp 'S' bend.
GPS: N50°12.752' W005°29.372'
OS grid: 203 SW 511 405

All Year

Trevalgan Touring Park

St Ives, Cornwall, TR26 3BJ
Tel: 01736 791892
www.trevalgantouringpark.co.uk

This is the sister site to the excellently located Ayr Holiday Park in St Ives and enjoys views across countryside to the sea from many pitches. Where Ayr is great for younger campers, this site is great for families and people wishing to relax and unwind. Both sites are immaculately kept with excellent facilities. The toilet and shower facilities at Trevalgan were refurbished in 2014. A bus stops on site from June-mid September taking campers the 2 miles to St Ives.

| NA 9 | NP 135 | 16 AMP |

Shop on site. Pub and beach 0.5 miles at St Ives.

££££

Directions: Exit A30 for St Ives. In 350m turn left at 2nd mini roundabout following signs to St Ives for heavy vehicles. In 3 miles turn right at T-Junction onto B3311. In 1 mile turn right at T-Junction onto B3306 towards St Ives. Travel 0.5 miles and turn right (brown tourist sign) to the campsite. Take the right fork in 0.5 miles, then drive 300m to the site.
GPS: N50°12.468' W005°31.136'
OS grid: 203 SW 490 401

May - September

Trevedra Farm Caravan and Camping Site `47`

Sennen, Penzance, Cornwall, TR19 7BE
Tel: 01736 871818
www.trevedrafarm.co.uk

Trevedra campsite has been family run for over 80 years and is part of a working farm. There are four camping areas, one for Caravan Club members, a peak season area with serviced pitches and two separate camping fields, one with direct access to the beach via a footpath. The facilities are modern and well cared for and there is an onsite shop and cafe. Sennen Cove and Gwenver sandy surf beaches are about 1 mile away and both have seasonal lifeguards in attendance. Land's End is also within walking distance along the South West Coast Path.

NA	12	NP	200	16 AMP		
WC					MG	MB

Shop and cafe on site. Pub and beach 1 mile at Sennen Cove.

££££ 🐕 †† M CL CS (i) WiFi

Directions: From Penzance travel southwest on A30, sp 'Land's End'. The site entrance is on the right 100m after the turning to St Just, clearly signed. Postcode not suitable for satnav.

GPS: N50°05.282' W005°40.735'
OS grid: 203 SW 369 274

April - October

Sennen Cove Camping and Caravanning Club Site `48`

Higher Tregiffian Farm, St Buryan, Penzance, Cornwall, TR19 6JB Tel: 01736 871588
www.campingandcaravanningclub.co.uk

This is a small, gently sloping, well maintained site. The sea can be seen over the hedges and attractive farmland. Walking to the beach takes you down a steep 1 mile path with steps. You can also walk to Land's End on the South West Coast Path, where there are pubs, restaurants and amusements. Aircraft noise can be heard on site, but can be appreciated if you take a scenic flight in a Cessna. See www.islesofscilly-travel.co.uk for information.

NA	3	NP	72	16 AMP		
WC					MG	MB

Pub and shop at St Just.

£££ 🐕 †† M CL CS (i) WiFi

Directions: From Penzance travel southwest on A30, sp 'Land's End'. In 6 miles turn right onto B3306, sp 'St Just'. After 200m turn left onto a private lane. The site is a few metres further on the left. Drivers who are towing should avoid driving into Sennen Cove.

VisitEngland
★★★★
TOURING & CAMPING PARK

GPS: N50°05.381' W005°40.150'
OS grid: 203 SW 378 276

April - October

Kenneggy Cove Holiday Park

Higher Kenneggy, Rosudgeon, Penzance,
Cornwall, TR20 9AU Tel: 01736 763453
www.kenneggycove.co.uk

Most pitches on this small, pleasant site enjoy sea views and electric hook-up, and both are bookable. Tranquillity is the name of the game with a policy of no noise after 10pm or before 8am. The tropical plants and landscaping create an attractive campsite during the season and a lovely garden when the site is closed. The facilities are immaculate and there is homemade food, including pizza, available from the onsite cafe. 0.25 miles down a natural footpath brings you to the South West Coast Path and Kenneggy Sands, a stunning, secluded beach.

NA	4	NP	50	16 AMP		
WC					MG	MB

££££ 🐕 ♀♂ M CL CS ⓘ WiFi

Directions: From A30 at the Newtown Roundabout turn onto A394 towards Helston. At the large blue 'Kenneggy Cove' sign turn right. Continue for 0.4 miles to the site.

VisitEngland
★★★★
HOLIDAY, TOURING & CAMPING PARK

GPS: N50°06.495' W005°24.735'
OS grid: 203 SW 562 286

Mid May - Mid October

Higher Pentreath Farm

Praa Sands, Penzance, Cornwall, TR20 9TL
Tel: 01736 763222

This site has not been ravaged by the modern world. Simple camping fields and basic facilities are all you need to enjoy this wonderful area. Stunning views are enjoyed from every camping field; the higher up you go the better the sea view and the quieter it gets. There is a 15 mins walk downhill to the beach.

NA	8	NP	100	10 AMP		
WC					MG	MB

Pub and beach 15 mins downhill.

£££ 🐕 ♀♂ M CL CS ⓘ WiFi

Directions: From A30 at the Newtown Roundabout turn onto A394 towards Helston. In 4.9 Miles turn right onto Penreath Lane, sp 'Penreath'. In 0.4 miles turn right into the site.

GPS: N50°06.480' W005°23.611'
OS grid: 203 SW 574 284

March - October

Bos Verbas CS

Helston Road, Germoe, Penzance, TR20 9AA
Tel: 01736 761873/07787 390269
www.bosverbas.com

© Site Owner

No twin axle   Max 7m

This small site is surrounded by farmland, but elevated enough for half of the pitches to enjoy sea views out across Praa Sands. 2 out of 3 small camping areas have sea views through trees and both shepherd's huts have private garden areas and lovely sea views. The overall feel of the site is like being in someone's back garden with good quality, homely facilities. Marazion is 4 miles away and from there you can visit the tidal island of St Michael's Mount with its castle and beautiful gardens. Praa Sands centre and sandy beach are just 1 mile away.

| NA 2.5 | NP 15 | 16 AMP | | |

| WC | | | | | | MG | MB |

Pub 1 mile at Praa Sands. Children's play area 4 miles at Marazion. Swimming pool 5 miles at Penzance.

££££ 🐕 ♂♀ M CL CS ⓘ WiFi

Directions: From Helston on A394 travel towards Newtown. 200m after Newtown Services fuel station turn left onto a private road. The site is signed here.

GPS: N50°06.772' W005°23.289'
OS grid: 203 SW 578 293

May - August

Chy Carne Camping and Touring

Kuggar, Ruan Minor, Helston, Cornwall,
TR12 7LX Tel: 01326 290200/291161
www.chycarne.co.uk

Half the touring pitches on this pleasant site have views of the sea. A mix of statics and camping facilities set within a sheltered, tree lined site combine to provide a safe, friendly and relaxing base from which to explore. The site is quiet and comfortable with great stargazing at night.

| NA 8 | NP 70 | 16 AMP | | |

| WC | | | | | | MG | MB |

Shop, pub and takeaway on site. Beach 5 mins.

££££ 🐕 ♂♀ M CL CS ⓘ WiFi

Directions: From Helston head south on A3083 towards Lizard Point. Travel through Penhale, then in 1.3 miles turn left, sp 'Kennack Sands'. In 1 mile turn left at the crossroads, sp 'Kenneck Sands'. Follow the road for 0.8 miles and the site is on the left once you enter Kuggar.

GPS: N50°00.258' W005°10.575'
OS grid: 204 SW 725 164

April - October

Trewince Farm

Portscatho, Truro, Cornwall, TR2 5ET
Tel: 01872 580430
www.trewincefarm.co.uk

This 5 acre campsite is part of a working farm. The site owners are charming and the site is lovely. Virtually every pitch offers views of the sea and those with obscured sea views have fantastic countryside views. This site is sloping, but there are many level pitches. 2 miles away, the pretty Cornish village of Postscartho has a sandy beach, slipway, pubs and restaurants. Towan Beach is within walking distance.

NA	5	NP	25	🎣 13 AMP		

Pub and shop 1 mile at Gorran.

£££

Directions: From St Austell on A390 towards Truro turn left onto B3287, sp 'Tregony'. Continue following sp 'Tregony', then after 4.5 miles turn left onto A3078, sp 'St Mawes'. In 6.1 miles turn left, sp 'St Anthony', 'Portscatho' and 'Gerrans'. The site is straight ahead in 2.2 miles, clearly signed.

GPS: N50°10.017' W004°59.224'
OS grid: 204 SW 866 339

May - September

Treloan Coastal Holidays

Treloan Lane, Gerrans, Portscatho, Truro, Cornwall, TR2 5EF Tel: 01872 580989
www.coastalfarmholidays.co.uk

Max 10m

There is not one, but three sandy coves within walking distance of this beautiful and scenic campsite. Campers have a choice of a eco-hut, a yurt, mobile homes, touring pitches or backpacking pitches, all spread across 3 acres. The site is keen on promoting responsible tourism, the local environment and local culture. It hosts artists, writers, foragers and many others who arrange activities for campers throughout the peak season. Portscatho, with its pubs, restaurants and sandy beach, is only 0.5 miles away and the South West Coast Path can be picked up just 400m from the edge of the site.

NA	3	NP	50	🎣 16 AMP		

Pub, shop, beach and children's play area 0.5 miles at Portscatho.

£££

Directions: From Truro on A390 travel northeast towards St Austell. In 5 miles turn right onto A3078, sp 'Tregony' and 'St Mawes'. At Trewithian turn left, sp 'Portscatho', 'Gerrans' and 'St Anthony'. After 1.4 miles turn left, then right onto Treloan Lane. The site is on the left in 200m.

GPS: N50°10.510' W004°58.760'
OS grid: 204 SW 874 348

All Year

Seaview International Holiday Park `55`

Boswinger, Gorran, St Austell, Cornwall, PL26 6LL Tel: 01726 843425
www.seaviewinternational.com

This is an exceptional campsite with excellent facilities and fully deserving of its five star status. Of the 189 touring pitches, only 7 have a good view of the sea, so advanced booking is necessary. The sea can also be seen from the pool and children's play area. There are sandy beaches on either side of the site. 0.75 miles to the east is Hemmick Beach, accessible down a very narrow road with no real parking area. Or 1.5 miles to the west is the larger Porthluney Beach, which has a large car park.

| NA | 8 | NP | 70 | 16 AMP | | |

| WC | | | | | MG | MB |

Beach 0.75 miles or 1.5 miles.

££££ 🐕 †† M CL CS ⓘ WiFi

Directions: From St Austell travel south on B3273, sp 'Mevagissey'. In 4.3 miles turn right, sp 'Portmellon avoiding weight limit'. After 4.4 miles turn right, sp 'Treveor', 'Boswinger' and 'Seaview International'. In 0.7 miles turn right, sp 'Seaview International'. The site is on the right in 0.4 miles, clearly signed.

GPS: N50°14.239' W004°49.143'
OS grid: 204 SW 990 411

April - September

Treveague Farm Campsite `56`

Gorran, St Austell, Cornwall PL26 6NY
Tel: 01726-842295
www.treveaguefarm.co.uk

Treveague is a family run, 200 acre, organic, working farm breeding sheep, cattle and pigs. The 4 acre, partly level campsite is on the brow of a hill, affording all pitches panoramic views across the rolling countryside and sea. Half the pitches are serviced. There are 3 well appointed cottages for hire and all guests are encouraged to interact with the farm animals and watch the wildlife from special hides. In peak season there is an onsite restaurant serving the farm's own produce, or you can buy the farm's produce from the onsite shop and cook it yourself.

| NA | 200 | NP | 80 | 16 AMP | | |

| WC | | | | | MG | MB |

Pub and shop 1 mile at Gorran Haven.

££££ 🐕 †† M CL CS ⓘ WiFi

Directions: From St Austell follow B3273 for 4.5 miles, then turn right, sp 'Lost Gardens of Heligan'. Follow road 5.5 miles, past the Lost Gardens and then following sp 'Treveague Farm'.

GPS: N50°14.311' W004°48.271'
OS grid: 204 SX 004 413

April - September

Pentewan Sands Holiday Park

Pentewan, Cornwall, PL26 6BT
Tel: 01726 843485
www.pentewansands.com

This large commercial site has everything including its own private sandy beach. The site is mainly level, so only the front row has excellent sea views, however from these 48 pitches you can literally roll out of bed and onto the beach, where there is a children's playground and designated swimming and boat areas. Pentewan village is 2 mins walk away and the Lost Gardens of Heligan are 2 miles uphill. Advance booking is essential in high season when pitches are available for weekly slots only.

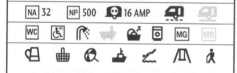

| NA 32 | NP 500 | 16 AMP |

££££

Directions: From St Austell take B3273 south for 3.7 miles. The site is adjacent to B3273 at Pentewan.

GPS: N50°17.289' W004°47.150'
OS grid: 204 SX 016 468

Easter - October

Penhale Caravan and Camping Park

Fowey, Cornwall, PL23 1JU
Tel: 01726 833425
www.penhale-fowey.co.uk

This family run campsite is part of Penhale organic farm. All pitches have beautiful views over gently rolling farmland and out over St Austell Bay. The majority of the touring pitches are level and have electric hook-up. In addition there is a basic camping field and 11 holiday homes for hire. A sandy beach and the South West Coast Path are 1 mile away in Polkerris and the historic town of Fowey is 1.5 miles away. The Fowey Royal Regatta, held every August, is quite a spectacle.

| NA 65 | NP 56 | 16 AMP |

Shop on site. Pub 1 mile. Beach and slipway 1 mile at Polkerris via footpath. Swimming pool 1.2 miles in Fowey.

£££

Directions: From Lostwithiel on A390 travel southwest towards St Austell. Turn left onto B3269, sp 'Fowey'. In 4.5 miles turn right at the roundabout onto A3082, sp 'St Austell'. The site is on the left in 0.5 miles.

GPS: N50°20.588' W004°40.098'
OS grid: 200 SX 101 526

March - October

West Wayland Touring Park [59]

West Wayland, Looe, Cornwall, PL13 2JS
Tel: 01503 262418
www.westwayland.co.uk

This is a beautifully kept campsite adjacent to the family farm. The grass is well maintained and unusually level. Most pitches offer views across the countryside to the sea. The owners take great pride in the site and the low tariffs represent excellent value for money. There is a beach about 1 mile away and the pretty seaside town of Looe, with numerous shops, restaurants, pubs and a sandy beach, is also close by.

| NA 20 | NP 120 | 16 AMP |

Shop on site. Pub 1 mile. Beach and slipway 1 mile via footpath at Polkerris. Swimming pool 1.2 miles in Fowey.

££££

Directions: From either direction on A38 turn onto A374 at the Trerulefoot Roundabout, sp 'Looe'. In 1.2 miles turn right onto A387, sp 'Looe'. After 3.2 miles continue straight onto B3253. In 3.3 miles continue onto A387, sp 'Looe'. In 2.6 miles the site is clearly signed on the left.

GPS: N50°21.187' W004°29.849'
OS grid: 200 SX 103 526

April - September

Bay View Farm Caravan and Camping Site [60]

St Martins, Looe, Cornwall, PL13 1NZ
Tel: 01503 265922/07967 267312
www.looebaycaravans.co.uk

Two things make this site exceptional: First, the entire site has a captivating sea view. The elevated position overlooking Looe Bay allows you to watch the daytime comings and goings of fishing boats, and to enjoy the nighttime reflection of the town lights on the water. Second, Mike, the owner, has a friendly, laid back approach, which creates a very special atmosphere enhanced by his friendly shire horses grazing in adjacent paddocks. Walk along the Coast Path to the beach or 1.5 miles to the pretty seaside town of Looe, famed for its daily fish market. Fishermen love it here as many charter boats offer everything from mackerel to shark fishing trips.

| NA 5 | NP 50 | 16 AMP |

Beach 0.25 miles via footpath. Pub, shop, slipway 1.5 miles (Coast Path) or 4.5 miles (by car) at Looe.

£££

Directions: From either direction on A38 turn onto A374 at the Trerulefoot Roundabout, sp 'Looe'. In 1.2 miles turn right onto A387, sp 'Looe'. After 3.2 miles continue straight onto B3253. In 1.2 miles, as you enter No Man's Land, turn left and follow sp 'Monkey Sanctuary'. At the Monkey Sanctuary bear right. The site is in 0.6 miles, clearly signed.

GPS: N50°21.824' W004°25.704'
OS grid: 201 SX 274 545

All Year

Mollie Tucker's Field *CL*

Higher House Farm, East Prawle, Kingsbridge, Devon, TQ7 2BU Tel: 01548 511422
www.caravanclub.co.uk

This *CL* is just 50m from the village green where there are two pubs, a shop, and a café, and Stephen's Field is also just around the corner. This is a buzzing place during the summer holidays with an August regatta, so you will need to pre book. Out of season you will be able to relax in peace and quiet and enjoy the wide open sea view.

| NA | 0.75 | NP | 5 | ☠ 16 AMP | | |

Pub and shop 50m. Beach 1.75 miles (Coast Path) or 3.75 miles (by car). Slipway 3.75 miles in East Portlemouth.

££££ 🐕 †† Ⓜ *CL* CS ⓘ WiFi

Directions: From Dartmouth travel south on A379 towards Kingsbridge. At the Carehouse Cross roundabout turn left, sp 'Beesands', 'Prawle' and 'E. Portlemouth'. Continue on this road following sp 'E. Prawle', then follow sp 'Prawle Point' through East Prawle village. The site is on left through a five bar gate, signed.

GPS: N50°12.871' W003°42.596'
OS grid: 202 SX 780 362

March - October

Stephen's Field

East Prawle, Kingsbridge, Devon, TQ7 2DF
Tel: 01548 511422

This August-only camping field has a good sea view, not quite as good as Mollie Tucker's Field which is almost adjacent, but this site will probably be the quietest when things are in full swing. It is also more sheltered from the southwest and you don't have to be a club member to stay here. There are toilets on site, but loo roll is not provided! There are also public toilets by the adjacent village green as well as two pubs, a shop, and a cafe. Pick up the South West Coast Path 1 mile away at Prawle Point.

| NA | 4 | NP | 25 | ☠ 0 AMP | | |

Shop, pub and cafe 60m. Showers are available at The Pigs Nose Inn.

££££ 🐕 †† Ⓜ *CL* CS ⓘ WiFi

Directions: From Dartmouth travel south on A379 towards Kingsbridge. At the Carehouse Cross roundabout turn left, sp 'Beesands', 'Prawle' and 'E. Portlemouth'. Continue on this road following sp 'E. Prawle', then follow sp 'Prawle Point' through East Prawle village. The site is at the back left-hand side of the village green, down an unmade road, sp 'Stephen's Field'.

GPS: N50°12.883' W003°42.593'
OS grid: 202 SX 780 362

August Only

Slapton Sands Camping and Caravanning Site | 63

Middle Grounds, Slapton, Kingsbridge, Devon, TQ7 2QW Tel: 01548 580538
www.campingandcaravanningclub.co.uk

Members only

This club site is lined with hedges and trees, which obscure much of the view of the long shingle beach and the amazing Slapton Ley; a long strip of fresh water just behind the beach. Caravan pitches are for members only, but non member motorhomes and tents are also welcome. The Ley is within a Nature Reserve and is a great place to observe wildlife or enjoy the many walking trails. The South West Coast Path is 0.5 miles downhill from the site, and from there you can walk to one of the sandy beaches at either end of the bay.

| NA | 3 | NP | 115 | 16 AMP | | |

Pub 0.25 miles. Shop and slipway 2 miles at Torcross.

£££ 🐕 †† M CL CS (i) WiFi

Directions: From Dartmouth travel south on A379 towards Kingsbridge. In 6.2 miles turn right, sp 'Slapton'. In 0.4 miles the site is on the right.

GPS: N50°17.439' W003°39.026'
OS grid: 202 SX 825 450

April - October

Leonards Cove Holiday Park | 64

New Road, Stoke Fleming, Dartmouth, South Devon, TQ6 0NR Tel: 01803 770206
www.leonardscove.co.uk

This is a beautiful, but basic site in an area of outstanding natural beauty. There are sea views from most of the tent pitches, but touring pitches are slightly higher up with more obstructed views. The statics at the front of the site enjoy fantastic views over open countryside to the sea. Blackpool Sands is a short meander away and the village of Stoke Fleming, with pubs and the campsite's own restaurant Radius 7, is just 100m up the road.

| NA | 1.5 | NP | 45 | 16 AMP | | |

Shop on site. Restaurant 120m. Pub 0.25 miles. Beach 0.5 miles at Blackpool Sands. Slipway 3 miles at Dartmouth.

££££ 🐕 †† M CL CS (i) WiFi

Directions: From Dartmouth travel south on A379 to Stoke Fleming. The site is on the left in 2.1 miles.

GPS: N50°19.367' W003°35.888'
OS grid: 202 SX 864 482

May - Mid September

Dartmouth Caravan and Camping Club Site

Dartmouth Road, Stoke Fleming, Dartmouth, Devon, TQ6 ORF Tel: 01803 770253
www.campingandcaravanningclub.co.uk

Max 9m

This well run site has limited sea views and the pitches are allocated on a first come, first served basis. All pitches have electric, the facilities are clean and the staff are friendly. With no clubhouse or bar, you may need to venture elsewhere for entertainment. Catch one of the hourly buses just outside the site, which will take you the 2.5 miles to Dartmouth where you can enjoy all of its amenities or cross the River Dart to Kingswear and catch a steam train along the picturesque route to Paignton.

NA 8	NP 90	16 AMP		

Pub 1 mile in Stoke Fleming. Swimming pool and slipway 1 mile in Dartmouth. Beach 2 miles at Blackpool Sands.

£££ WiFi

Directions: From Dartmouth travel south on A379 for 1.5 miles. The site is clearly signed on the right.

GPS: N50°19.875' W003°35.790'
OS grid: 202 SX 864 492

Easter - Mid October

Hillhead Caravan Club Site

Hillhead, Brixham, Devon, TQ5 0HH
Tel: 01803 853204
www.caravanclub.co.uk

Max 9m

Few pitches have a view of the sea, but this is an exceptional site. Hedged terraced areas create a secluded feel. Many of the pitches are serviced hardstandings. The communal facilities are second to none and there is a great children's castellated play area. Mansands Beach is a vigorous 2.5 miles downhill walk.

NA 22	NP 256	16 AMP		

Shop, bar and restaurant on site. Beach 1.5 miles.

£££ WiFi

Directions: At Hillhead turn off A379 onto B3205, sp 'Kingswear', 'Dartmouth', and 'Lower Ferry'. Follow the road for 220m and the site is on the left, clearly signed.

GPS: N50°22.207' W003°32.696'
OS grid: 202 SX 904 534

March - January

Beverley Park Caravan & Camping Site `67`

Goodrington Road, Paignton, Devon,
TQ4 7JE Tel: 01803 661961
www.beverley-holidays.co.uk

This is a family orientated holiday complex with lots of excellent facilities and plenty of static caravans for hire. There are plenty of camping pitches, but the area with the best sea views is gently sloping. The Upperdeck Bar has an outside terrace overlooking the large heated outdoor pool and camping fields onto the sea and the English Riviera. Everywhere is very well kept and clean.

| NA 20 | NP 180 | ☠ 16 AMP | 🚐 | 🚐 |

| WC | ♿ | 🚿 | 🛁 | 🧺 | ▣ | MG | MB |

🔌 🧺 🔍 ⛴ 🏊 🛝 🚶

££££ 🐕 👫 M CL CS ⓘ WiFi

Directions: From Paignton travel south on A3022, sp 'Brixham' and 'Kingswear'. In 1 mile turn left at the traffic lights, sp 'Goodrington Post Office' and 'Holiday Parks'. In 0.5 miles turn right into the site, clearly signed.

GPS: N50°24.828' W003°34.117'
OS grid: 202 SX 886 582

All Year

Ladram Bay Holiday Park `68`

Otterton, Budleigh Salterton, Devon,
EX9 7BX Tel: 01395 568398
www.ladrambay.co.uk

This is a one stop holiday spot. Remotely located, this is a large, family owned site with lots of quality accommodation and excellent facilities, like underfloor heating in the amenity block, an indoor pool, sauna and jacuzzi. You could come here for a week and feel no need to leave site. The private shingle beach is stunning and there is a slipway to the beach with boat storage adjacent. The terraced camping fields have fantastic sea views from most pitches. Indeed, sea views can be seen from most places, but the bar/restaurant terrace has the best. There is a very well stocked shop, fantastic children's entertainment, and it is directly on the South West Coast Path.

| NA 20 | NP 200 | ☠ 16 AMP | 🚐 | 🚐 |

| WC | ♿ | 🚿 | 🛁 | 🧺 | ▣ | MG | MB |

🔌 🧺 🔍 ⛴ 🏊 🛝 🚶

££££ 🐕 👫 M CL CS ⓘ WiFi

Directions: Turn off B3052 onto B3178, sp 'Budleigh Salterton'. Turn off into Otterton, sp 'Ladram Bay' and 'Camping'. Follow signs to Ladram Bay.

GPS: N50°39.709' W003°17.136'
OS grid: 192 SY 096 851

March - October

Salcombe Regis Camping and Caravan Park [69]

Salcombe Regis, Sidmouth, Devon,
EX10 0JH Tel: 01395 514303
www.salcombe-regis.co.uk

This is a gorgeous, medium sized site that really offers quality camping in every aspect. Unfortunately, only a handful of tent pitches benefit from the wonderful valley and sea view. The park and its facilities are kept immaculately. Sidmouth, about 10 mins drive away, retains its Regency and Victorian elegance, and boasts two pebble beaches which, at low tide, give way to golden sand and rock pools.

| NA | 16 | NP | 100 | 10 AMP | | |

| WC | | | | | MG | MB |

£££

Directions: At Hillhead turn off A379 onto B3205, sp 'Kingswear', 'Dartmouth', and 'Lower Ferry'. Follow the road for 220m and the site is on the left, clearly signed.

GPS: N50°41.743' W003°12.307'
OS grid: 192 SY 149 892

Easter - October

Manor Farm Caravan & Camping Site [70]

Seaton Down Road, Seaton, Devon, EX12 2JA
Tel: 01297 21524
www.manorfarmcaravansite.com

Wherever you pitch on this well laid out farm site, you are almost guaranteed a great view over Seaton to the bay beyond. The site is sloping, but most pitches are level. In addition to the touring and camping pitches, there are 200 seasonal pitches. There is plenty for children to enjoy, they can help feed the farm animals, cuddle Rocky - the farm's pet raccoon, or play in the enclosed playground. Seaton Esplanade and stony beach are 1 mile away and you can ride the narrow-gauge Seaton Tramway 3 miles through the Axe Valley to Colyton.

| NA | 22 | NP | 28 | 10 AMP | | |

| WC | | | | | MG | MB |

Shop on site. Pub, slipway and beach 1 mile at Seaton.

£££

Directions: From Lyme Regis follow A3052 west towards Exeter. After 7 miles turn left onto B3178, sp 'Seaton'. The site is on the right in 0.5 miles.

GPS: N50°42.840' W003°05.073'
OS grid: 193 SY 236 913

Mid March - Mid November

Seadown Holiday Park

Bridge Road, Charmouth, Dorset, DT6 6QS
Tel: 01297 561130
www.seadownholidaypark.co.uk

This site offers peace and relaxation. Although the sea and sandy beach are just 0.5 miles away, the site has sea glimpses only. In addition to the touring and camping pitches, there are also 70 statics for hire. The location is great because there are village amenities on one side and open countryside and the River Char on the other. You can walk down the Char to Charmouth Beach, and during low tide continue 3 miles along the beach to Lyme Regis.

NA 14   NP 54   16 AMP

WC   MG   MB

Shop on site. Pub 360m at Charmouth. Slipway at Lyme Regis. Swimming pool 5 miles at Axminster.

££££   M   CL CS   i   WiFi

Directions: From Bridport on A35 travel west for 5.8 miles. Take the Charmouth exit, then in 0.5 miles turn left onto Bridge Road. The site is in 100m, entrance clearly visible.

GPS: N50°44.271' W002°53.864'
OS grid: 193 SY 367 933

Mid March - October

Golden Cap

Seatown, Chideock, Bridport, Dorset, DT6 6JX Tel: 01308 422139
www.wdlh.co.uk

This site is located perfectly for a beach holiday as there is easy access to the shingle beach, which is only 100m away. Unfortunately, only a handful of pitches have a good sea view and advanced booking is required. There are glimpses of the sea in some other areas, but there are good views of the surrounding hills almost everywhere. Pitches are well defined with plenty of shrubs and trees breaking up the site. Levelling blocks are supplied where required and some areas are a little cosy. A modern toilet block is provided.

NA 154   NP 108   10 AMP

WC   MG   MB

Small shop on site. Pub and beach 100m. Slipway 5 miles at Charmouth or West Bay.

££££   M   CL CS   i   WiFi

Directions: On A35 between Dorchester and Honiton turn off at Chideock opposite the church onto Duck Street, sp 'Seatown'. The site entrance is on the left in 0.7 miles.

GPS: N50°43.415' W002°49.325'
OS grid: 193 SY 423 920

March - October

Highlands End Holiday Park

Eype, Bridport, Dorset, DT6 6AR
Tel: 01308 422139
http://highlandsendholidaypark.co.uk

This site oozes a quality and refinement that you can sense as you come down the drive. The camping fields offer exceptional views, some over rolling hills, some over the cliffs to the sea. There are 39 serviced pitches. The bar has wonderful old Royal Berkshire fire engines on display and there is also a cafe and a formal restaurant. The onsite Leisure Club has a swimming pool, tennis court and 9-hole pitch and putt golf course (extra charges apply). Join the South West Coast Path at the end of the park for beautiful walks along beaches and clifftops. The shingle beach is just 500m downhill.

| NA 27 | NP 192 | 10 AMP | | |

| WC | | | | | | MG | MB |

Pub, shop and restaurant on site. Pub, shop and beach 2 miles at West Bay.

££££ M CL CS WiFi

Directions: From Bridport follow A35 southwest and turn off, sp 'Eype'. Follow this road and take the 4th right turning to the site entrance, clearly signed. Follow road to reception.

GPS: N50°43.430' W002°46.734'
OS grid: 193 SY 452 913

March - October

Eype House Caravan and Camping Park

Eype, Bridport, Dorset, DT6 6AL
Tel: 01308 424903
www.eypehouse.co.uk

Approached down a very narrow, high-hedged lane, this lovely south facing, steeply sloping, terraced site is only suitable for tents and small campervans. The elevated location provides excellent views from every pitch, down to the beach and along a section of the Jurassic coast. There are static caravans for hire below the tent pitches. The pebble beach is a 200m downhill walk with 14 steps along the path.

| NA 4.5 | NP 20 | 0 AMP | | |

| WC | | | | | | MG | MB |

Pub, shop, beach and slipway at West Bay.

££££ M CL CS WiFi

Directions: This site is not licensed for touring caravans. 1.25 miles West of Bridport on A35. Take the turning south to Eype and drive through the village towards the sea.

GPS: N50°43.090' W002°47.013'
OS grid: 193 SY 446 912

All Year

West Bay Holiday Park

West Bay, Bridport, Dorset, DT6 4HB
Tel: 01308 459491
www.parkdean.com/westbay

Max 8.5m

This large site is laid out alongside the River Brit and adjacent to West Bay harbour. The majority of the site is occupied by statics. Touring pitches are laid out on terraces above affording them views over the river, the town and the sea in the distance. There are tons of facilities and entertainment for all ages on site, including an arcade and indoor swimming pool with flume. Catch a fishing trip from the harbour or hire a bicycle on site and explore the Jurassic coastline along the South West Coast Path which is right on your doorstep.

| NA 30 | NP 116 | 10/16 AMP | | |

Pub, shop, swimming pool and arcade on site. Beach 100m.

£££ WiFi

Directions: From Dorchester on A35 travel west towards Honiton. In 12.7 miles turn left at the roundabout, sp 'Honiton' and 'Exeter'. In 0.7 miles go straight on at the roundabout onto B3157, sp 'West Bay'. In 0.8 miles go straight on at the 1st roundabout, then turn right at the 2nd roundabout into the site.

GPS: N50°42.713' W002°45.819'
OS grid: 194 SY 461 907

Mid March - Mid November

Bagwell Farm Touring Park

Chickerell, Weymouth, Dorset, DT3 4EA
Tel: 01305 782575
www.bagwellfarm.co.uk

Max 12m

This friendly farm site offers the best of both worlds. Sitting on a hill surrounded by farmland, you get the tranquillity of the countryside with beautiful views over the Fleet and famous Chesil Beach. There are great views from the whole site, except for the lower tent field which is sheltered by hedges. There is a mix of grass, gravel, fully serviced and seasonal pitches. The facilities are extremely well kept. The village of Chickerell is 1 mile away or you can travel a little further, 4.5 miles, for all the seaside amenities of Weymouth.

| NA 33 | NP 320 | 10/16 AMP | | |

Shop and restaurant on site. Pub 0.5 miles at Chickerell. Beach and swimming pool 4.5 miles at Weymouth.

£££ WiFi

Directions: From Weymouth on B3157 travel west towards Chickerell. In 0.7 miles turn right at the crossroads, sp 'Abbotsbury' and 'Chickerell'. Turn right at the roundabout, sp 'Abbotsbury' and 'Chickerell'. The site is on the left in 1 mile.

GPS: N50°38.087' W002°31.619'
OS grid: 194 SY 625 816

All Year

Littlesea Holiday Park

Lynch Lane, Weymouth, Dorset, DT4 9DT
Tel: 01305 774414
www.haven.com/parks/dorset/littlesea

Max 9m

This large Haven resort looks out over the West Dorset Heritage Coast to the Fleet and Chesil Beach. All that you would expect from a large commercial site is available here, including a large bar/restaurant, adventure golf, multiple swimming pools and lots of fun for kids. The site runs right up to the edge of the Fleet where it also meets the South West Coast Path. Visit Weymouth for the day, 2 miles, or take a walk along Chesil Beach onto the Isle of Portland and visit its 450 year old coastal fort built for Henry VIII.

NA	60	NP	150	16 AMP		
WC					MG	MB

Bar/restaurant on site. Beach and slipway 2.5 miles at Weymouth.

££££ 🐕 †† Ⓜ CL CS ⓘ WiFi

Directions: From Weymouth on B3157 travel west towards Chickerell. In 0.6 miles turn left at the roundabout, sp 'Portland' and 'Crematorium'. In 0.9 miles turn right, then immediately left, sp 'Lynch Industrial Estate'. The site is at the end of the road.

GPS: N50°36.372' W002°29.441'
OS grid: 194 SY 652 783

Easter - October

Pebble Bank Holiday Park

90 Camp Road, Wyke Regis, Weymouth, Dorset, DT4 9HF Tel: 01305 774844
www.pebblebank.co.uk

Adjacent to Chesil Beach, this is a homely and comfortable site. The 1 acre tent field at the top of the site has spectacular views across Portland. Tourers have their own small, pine tree edged, partly sloping area overlooking the Fleet, fishermen's huts, and Chesil Beach. Access to the Fleet is 100m. There are 100 static caravans, some are privately owned and some are available to rent.

NA	5	NP	40	10 AMP		
WC					MG	MB

Pub/restaurant on site. Pub and shop 1 mile at Old Wyke. Beach and slipway 2 miles at Weymouth.

££££ 🐕 †† Ⓜ CL CS ⓘ WiFi

Directions: From Weymouth on A354 towards Portland, turn right at the crossroads by the Rodwell pub into Wyke Road. Continue for 1 mile, then turn left onto Camp Road, sp 'Superstore' and 'Garden centre'. After 400m turn left into the site, clearly signed.

GPS: N50°35.778' W002°29.286'
OS grid: 194 SY 657 776

April - October

East Fleet Farm Touring Park

Fleet Lane, Chickerell, Weymouth, Dorset,
DT3 4DW Tel: 01305 785768
www.eastfleet.co.uk

This large, quiet, mainly sloping site is part of a 200 acre organic farm and has stunning views of The Fleet and Chesil Beach. The facilities are modern and very clean. Local food vendors visit the site selling pizza, fish and chips and wild boar burgers, and you can eat it in the comfort of The Old Barn, which is a beer lover's paradise. Meet up with the South West Coast Path at the bottom of the site and follow it along the Fleet, which is a great place to observe birds and wildlife.

NA 21   NP 380   10/16 AMP

WC   MG   MB

Shop and bar on site. Beach 3 miles at Weymouth.

£££ WiFi

Directions: From Weymouth on B3157 travel west towards Chickerell. In 0.7 miles continue straight at the crossroads, sp 'East Fleet' with the campsite symbol. In 0.6 miles turn left into the site.

GPS: N50°36.984' W002°30.717'
OS grid: 194 SY 640 797

Mid March - October

Durdle Door Holiday Park

Lulworth Cove, Wareham, Dorset, BH20 5PU
Tel: 01929 400200
www.lulworth.com

This is one of the few places on this section of coast where there is access to the sea, and many day visitors take advantage of this. There are plenty of non sea view pitches, including a very pleasant area under pine trees which is ideal during hot spells. A single row of pitches set back from the cliff provides the few sea view pitches available. However, most of these are so steep that only touring caravans can level by perching on concrete blocks. Unfortunately, day parking spoils the tranquillity and attractive views.

NA 45   NP 108   16 AMP

WC   MG   MB

Bar/restaurant and shop on site. Slipway 1.5 miles at Lulworth Cove.

£££ WiFi

Directions: From Ringwood on A31 travel west towards Bere Regis. At the roundabout turn left onto A35, sp 'Bournemouth' and 'Poole'. In 0.4 miles turn right at the roundabout, sp 'Bere Regis', 'Bovington' and 'Wool'. Continue for 5 miles, then turn right at the roundabout onto A352, sp 'Dorchester and 'Wool'. After 3.1 miles turn left, sp 'Winfrith Newburgh' and 'East Chaldon'. In 3.1 miles the site is on your right, clearly signed.

VisitEngland
★★★★
HOLIDAY, TOURING
& CAMPING PARK

GPS: N50°37.612' W002°16.096'
OS grid: 194 SY 812 809

March - October

Hurst View Leisure

Lower Pennington Lane, Pennington, Lymington, Hampshire, SO41 8AL Tel: 01590 671648
www.hurstviewleisure.co.uk

Blue Anchor, Somerset

This spacious site is spread across 4 level fields. One field has a distant sea view obscured by the sea wall. The path along the sea wall offers a better vantage point to enjoy the views across the Solent to the Isle of Wight. The site lies within the New Forest on a coastal reserve with ancient oak woods, estuaries and salt marshes which are great for bird watching. Lymington, 2 miles, is a Georgian market town with two large marinas, numerous commerce and an open-air sea water swimming bath.

Buckets and Spades, Woolacombe, Devon

| NA | 20 | NP | 200 | 16 AMP | | |

| WC | | | | | MG | MB |

Shop on site. Pub 1.7 miles. Beach 2 miles at Milford on Sea.

£££

WiFi

Barbecue, Weymouth, Dorset

Directions: From Lymington head south on A337 towards New Milton. At roundabout by Shell fuel station turn left, then immediately right, sp 'Hurst View'. Campsite entrance in 1 mile.

GPS: N50°44.219' W001°33.000'
OS grid: 195 SZ 318 929

All Year

Heather on Exmoor, Devon

Lizard Point, Cornwall

Coastal footpath to Watchet, Somerset

Uphill Marine Centre, Weston-super-Mare

Sunset from North Hill, Somerset